by Linda Cernak
illustrated by Kristin Sorra

Orlando Boston Dallas Chicago San Diego

Visit *The Learning Site!*
www.harcourtschool.com

When you go out your door, you can see birds roaming everywhere. What a show!

Birds use their bills to help them get food. Each bird has its own kind of bill. A bird bill is also called a *beak*.

Some birds eat seeds. This bird has a short, strong bill. It helps the bird crack the seeds.

Some birds eat bugs. This
bird looks for food near a road.
It uses its bill to eat bugs
that hide.

This bird has a sharp bill.
It's good for eating bugs in
tree bark.

Think and Respond

1. Are all bird bills the same?
2. How does a duck use its bill?
3. What kinds of things do some birds eat?
4. What do you think a bird with a long, sharp bill might eat?
5. Which kind of bird do you like the best? Tell why.

My Bird Book Find pictures of birds. Cut them out and paste them in a bird book. Tell what things the birds might eat.

School-Home Connection Go on a nature hike with a family member. Look for different kinds of birds. Describe the birds and the kinds of bills they have.

Word Count: 221

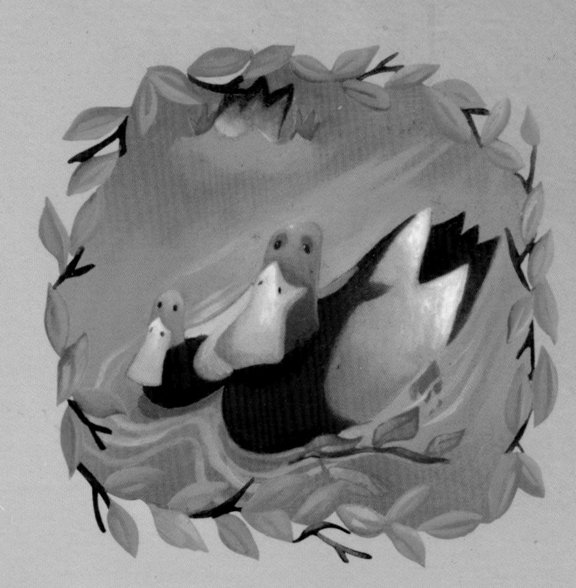

ISBN 0-15-323024-X
90000>
9 780153 230240

Some birds eat plants. This bird has a long, flat bill. It helps the bird eat plants that float.

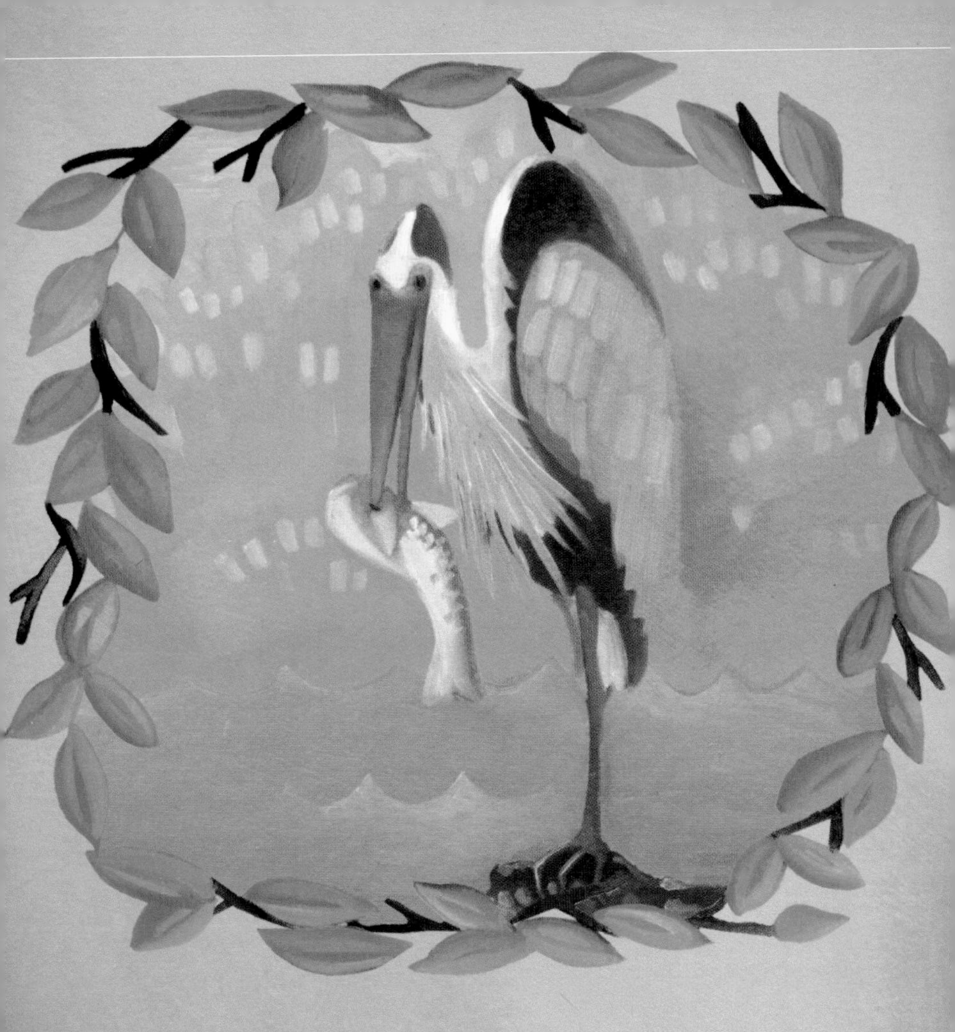

Some birds eat fish. This bird has a long, pointed bill. It is just right for catching fish!

This bird eats fruit. Its yellow bill is very long. The bird uses its bill to grab fruit from tree branches.

This little bird sips nectar from flowers. Its long, thin bill fits right into the flower.

This bird made her nest. Now she gives the baby birds food so they will grow. Who would think birds use their beaks in so many ways?

These people give the birds oats and bits of toast from bowls. Be kind to the birds you see. They are our friends.